Silver Hare Tales

Lauren Thomas

blood moon POETRY

Cover art by Maja Trolle
ISBN: 978-1-7399155-2-0
Imprint: blood moon POETRY

for Amelie and Thea

Note from the Editor:

When Lauren told me she had a manuscript ready to be published it was right at the start of our print publishing journey. We were excited but also knew we had a lot to learn; our digital journals had wildly exceeded our expectations and fed an appetite for poetry written by women that even we hadn't anticipated. So I was waiting for the right collection to find us, one that would embody the part of our small press that sought to uncover hidden poetic gems.

When I sat down to read Lauren's work, I felt like I was unearthing something really special. The poems you will read here feel warmed by her hands and will leave you with an urge to reconnect with whichever wild land you were formed from. This is a collection of stories passed down through generations of women, re-tellings of grief and loss, family rituals reimagined and glimpses into the wild and beautiful landscape of mothering.

As women we are often taught to walk through our lives disembodied and detached. Rooted women rise with power, and so it stands to reason that a society shaped by patriarchal values would benefit from helping us forget this truth.

Silver Hare Tales holds within it Lauren's exploration of her heritage; an ancestry shaped by geography, these poems are the maps written on her return. She acknowledges both generational histories and her own personal life experiences with gentle but evocative imagery. When I read her words I am transported and reminded that a woman who knows herself is a force to be reckoned with.

I will keep Silver Hare Tales on the small reading table by the fireplace in my living room. It will keep me company as I stoke the flames of my own desire to both return to and discover my womanhood.

Lunar love,

Holly Ruskin
Editor-in-chief & co-founder
blood moon POETRY

Note from the Author:

In this sequence of poems, I was focused on the importance of the natural world and its connection to self-identity. Having grown up in England rather than my family's homeland of South Wales, I have often found that themes of displacement and lineage run through my writing and that my connection to the natural world gives me a language to explore these ideas. Silver Hare Tales references childhood memories, formative experiences and the changing nature of relationships over time.

The first section, Roots, explores the idea of examining the past to find certainty in the present. Re-imagining a family history through the stories of four generations of women leads to a consideration of the ways in which story-telling and mythologising the past can bring unexpected clarity in the search for personal truths. I am interested in how stories, passed through generations of women, highlight not only their differences but also the things that connect them through the re-telling of personal histories. Whilst exploring generational differences in the way grief and loss are navigated, I also un-earthed unexpected connections underpinning the mother-daughter dynamics in these pieces.

The second section, Marrow, reflects on formative events that shape us as we grow, some of which might prematurely remove us from a place of comfort and innocence. When I moved to Wales in my late teens, I was faced with forging my own relationship with a place that I had romanticised all my life, a place that had always been there to dip in and out of, silvered by the people I loved. A place that was the backdrop to the few family rituals we had, and a place that I held close as part of my identity in the way we hold our most treasured memories close. I had lived other people's experiences of the place, and the reality of what happened to me there, changed me and my relationship with it forever. I fell even more in love with this landscape that I was so intrinsically connected to, but it also showed me its dark side, as life is want to do.

The final section, Clay, takes on a reflective tone and documents the difficulties of evolving relationships over time. As I watch my children grow I am also interested in the changing nature of relationships with others —the things we have to let go of. Ultimately, Silver Hare Tales ends on a note of acceptance and a return to the enriching capacity of the natural environment. The Welsh landscape, a constant in the poetry, reflects the texture and colour, the beauty and the bleakness that we may experience in the search for self-knowledge.

The Silver Hare serves as a glimpse into the universal wilderness of human existence, the meaningful connections and sense of belonging that we chase.

Contents

Roots

15 To My Country on Our National Day
19 Crynant 1939
21 Leaving St Flora's
23 A Family History
25 Garden's End
27 The Drowners
29 Just before
31 A Child

Marrow

33 A Road Away From Home
35 Silver Hare Tale
39 Bird
41 Mexican Night at the Union Bar
43 Tip 7
45 Bodyless
47 Flood
49 Funeral
51 A Winter's Morning

Clay

53 After Katrina, New Orleans 2016
55 Ysbyty Ifan
57 Hatton Flight
59 Reflections
61 Homing
63 Hiraeth
65 My Native Land Goodnight

Foreword

Occasionally I come across a poem, or poet which takes me back to the start and reminds me why I fell in love with this particular form of literature. A piece of writing that changes me, moves me, or makes me think. Words that lift me out of my everyday and immerse me in the elsewhere.

When I first read "Crynant, 1939" I felt the hairs on the back of my neck stand up and an image slowly start to paint itself in my mind. I felt moved and connected to an experience that I had never had, a place that I had never been to. This is the magic and skill of Lauren Thomas. Through her writing she connects and transports us to landscapes and experiences far outside of our own. We escape into a mystical place, where the past blurs into the present and our own experiences intertwine with hers.

There is a melancholy tone to this collection which I find incredibly moving, both as a writer and a mother. Growing up and now raising my own children in the countryside I can really relate to the way she speaks about her connection to the natural world. How it can hold us at different stages in our lives and how our relationships with it might alter over time. How these spaces and places reflect and echo our own experience through things like rebirth, restoration, or decay and how we then hand these landscapes down in memories and stories.

I adore the subtle, yet powerful undertone of womanhood throughout. A quiet questioning and turning over of different life stages. Like Lauren is writing to understand, to process and move forwards, which so many of us use poetry to do. Her writing is multilayered and uniquely descriptive, we walk with her through an emotional and physical space, gently nudged by her words to take a moment and reflect on our own sense of self and belonging.

As a female writer I feel empowered by collections like this one and female focused publishers like blood moon POETRY. They are unashamedly speaking about the reality of what it is to be a woman right now. Giving voice to and shining the spotlight on so many things that have been squashed or unspoken for far too long. Bringing high quality female writing to the fore and letting us all share in its wonder.

It feels collaborative. We are connecting through words, bonding over experiences, and championing each other. Holding political and social issues up and unacceptable behaviours to account. Sharing the truth without apology. I am proud to be a part of that.

I hope you enjoy this collection.

Kate Phipps
Writer & Founder of @katephippswrites
www.katephippswrites.com

Roots

To My Country

All my life I have been
turquoise eggs hidden in hedgerow,
waiting for you to discover me,
to turn me over in your hands,

compare my shell
to the wild birds in our garden.
On this yellow day
of bloom, I think of being bound

to you, with one foot in,
one foot out of your shores.
The dark frown of Port Talbot
asserts its orange steel shadow,

your sea-stripped
blue-earth desert,
red rust in your skin.
Your heather mountain summers,

are not mine.
Ruined abbey ghosts
flicker on the boundary
of my faded town.

Once, I was gifted a spoon,
a tiny carving—love,
spoken in Welsh wood, sung
by the tongues, the wax feather voices,

of the past. I will keep it
in moss-hushed space. I will keep it,
where I keep the wonder of a folly
on a green laced bank,

each soft-light, smelted silver ore,
reaching up from the valley on lost nights,
watched by my longing eye. Memories
threaded—beads on a rosary, oysters on rope.

I hold them, touch them,
like a little girl without a mother,
tracing the scarred backs of trees
to find the path that's hers.

Crynant, 1939

Her sleeves are rolled.
Knuckles red, she scrubs
the step, each inch, with suds.

This air is shoe polish and creosote,
hardware in the fibre and ligament,
brown bristle to the valley.

A Sunday child passes with morning,
reminds her of seclusion,
the Queen's black ribbons.

Probably best, they had said, the tiny death
scoured away. She had been too old
for step-scrub grief—she is younger now.

It is felt in the rain of this place,
the clink and hitch of allotment folk,
the bone felt urge to dig.

Leaving St Flora's

Standing on the gravel drive,
in the shadow of the house,
— its empty windowed height.
The wind, not sure
if it should blow,
understands the moment
and begins.

Far off, we hear
fragments of voices
swept in from sea,
laughter,
        cut off
middle   blotted out,
as if through an antique wireless,
grasping at wavelengths.

I breathe in sound.
Seagulls, delirious in screech,
the roar of air
in sycamore trees,
in the avenue over the wall,
their helicopter seeds   in spin,
purple wallflowers
open-bloomed   in disbelief.

Here it was left,
laid down in memorial,
buried
in the orange evening light
of the garden,
just beside the rockery
full of bees,
it's stone lion fountain
trickling forever on.

A Family History

We went by train to Wales.
The air got darker the deeper we went
through tunnels under the river.
A disturbance of light
brought on thoughts of your mother[1]
in pudding steamed aprons
and crinoline skirts.
Now she is sediment,
now she is fossil.[2]

Rain blurred the valley lights,
drawn from sea —remnants
of winter storms, ammonites preserved
in amber. Anne[3] had run up the hill
to tell them her news,[4]
the air awash with sea-mist streams,
the shimmer of slate, rushing water,
until —the whole place seemed to be
running down the hills in land-slipped,
full- mouthed song.
Stood in your kitchen—the knife
pointed upwards, you heard her run past,
raw bacon, on the counter in front of you[5].
Outside, the village was a tiny victorian funeral
— in a specimen jar.

As we were nearing the light,
I thought of sunny days at the Gower,
teenage ghosts of parents,
my mother's hip bones, cheek bones, [6]
She is poised—
like one of O'Keeffe's lilies, an arm curating her.
We resurface into sun, unearthed like a relic.
— Your seat is empty[7]

1 Her face, an exhibit of salt,
2 Eroding under this body of water.
3 Your daughter,
4 instead of you,
5 as if you'd divided up parts of yourself.
6 pieces of modern art.
7 -glass refracts light.

Garden's End

Once I found a fallen body
under leaves, beneath the pear,

kneeling at the garden's end
with others in the dark.

I'd always feared those shadow trees,
the tenet of their bark,

their hard rust fruit with nothing
but the pull and barb of wasps

and browning apples bruised
and thick with slugs.

I shifted on the ancient moss,
regarded the sharp ends of grass.

Her wings were spread as if to touch
the purple edges of this place.

Eyelids closed, her slowing breath,
holding less than songs.

I put her in a cardboard box
offered up the vivid pink umbilic twists

of worms. Murmured drops of milk
as words, whispered less than prayers.

Far away my mother's voice, calling
to the garden's end.

I thought of salvaging our lost
and sunlight trapped inside green glass.

The Drowners

A snap of wind invokes memories of your head cracking on the dresser.
Hands felt skull, felt wet black droplets. Breeze mothered
your closed red lids

After, we ran into the garden,
hot feet swiping,
damp   cool   grass.
Outside, the world was disaster.
We flung soft bodies
against the orange rust frame,
climbed right to the top
waving arms,
two drowners, slipping,
                        through fleeing water.
We dared the storm
white teeth against rain,
as it started,
ushered in like trapped blood
spreading under the skin of sky.
You were sideways with the horizon,
the yellow air flexed
  — held the split in x-ray.
We dared the storm again
and the world was   strung up
livid   blue   as its voice
smashed around us

When I looked up a green perfume bottle was mid fall
its shape like something I imagined from the Emerald City.
And so, I ran.

Just Before: *Blackdown Clinic*

The day has turned its back to me.
Eye squeeze pinks my tender blur,
Tucked away like a dismantled lamb.

Green curtains, robe my bleating fear,
Spins cold-breath cloth against
My teen-sculpt spine and plastic chair.

This room is dressed for death.
For some to wait. For some to run.
I didn't think I would be holding on for it.

A Child

Bird song and seaweed in its
dark green ribbons

evidence of storms that came
from deep inside the night

But here she patters in pools
and breeze blown ridges

Sea reflecting skim-stone sky above
its curling arms of deep just out

of reach. A quiet wild, held in sharp
sting of salt. Patterns in the sand

map the tidal pull and draw, the
white foam follows where she hops

from sturdy water-break to shore
oystered in her blue-boned wilderness

Marrow

A Road Away From Home

Time has brought me back to tread this green-silk road,
but 20 years have grown into the cracks and plotted lines,
that mapped my travels through these heavy hills,
like a welkin's shadow rooting through my country's brow.

We drive to Cardiff for a gig – just to buy a ticket from a spit
and sawdust pub. And folded neatly in my lap is all my artless
love, for you. This road was steel-work shadow-slip that led
me off to you, my back turned from the pleading coast,

closed off the rush of sea and carried me to where the scattered
air was twinkled blue —with valley lights of new and hot-mouthed love.
The last time I was on its path, I heard time's murmur in the darkness
shift   and at the heels of youth   I had to part with it.

As a child, I used to think that fairies lived in Castell Coch
and cry as we drove past, before I knew what had been lost.

Silver Hare Tale

This place was gifted to me
by your rose scented hands.
Its bright story words carried

as amulets through fluted valleys,
velvet dusk graveyards,
running fingers over old bones,
our soil and family grain.

Later, on sun-slipped mornings,
I lived on coastal glimmer
inside salt-sharp haze. The blue jolt
of new love on my tongue.

Later still, looking back
along the Mumbles shoreline,
a blur of your men,
your should-be fathers

and would-be sons,
songs of stone and boulder.
My borrowed land
lies in shadow.

It is the dark fury of a mother
and I have built a wall,
left the sea's-edge open,
like a child's wish,

a silver hare,
running the horizon.
The black rain that picks
at the hillside,

cannot write my tale
on cold-scratch slate.

The fading light
is someone else's to behold.

I hide from this country
inside its heirloom voice.
Its waters running through me,
its tongue, cool green moss

against my skin.
My mouth a stone circle,
words to be held   never
to be told as my own.

Bird

"Dawn. Not much light, mind.
A wavering sun has clambered
to the top of Brynmill.
Clatter-down houses up here,
taunt the town, down there,
breathing with the sea below.
Ethereal, from some views,
but really, its nicotined glass.
If you didn't know what was behind,
you'd think us boys were set for life.
Friends on tap, pub just b'there,
the pulsing current of Upland's fare.
But—as fresh and as free and as far away
as I felt from all of that and then,
I couldn't bring myself to stay,
or to see, what that town could bring to me.
And so I stepped
with bracing grief
Off towards those silver tips of sea.
Southerndown.
There she stood.
With cliffs that told a different way,
with rocks that seemed to offer me
the violence of my blame.
And when they came to see the place,
to hear that Laleston tale of mine,
in the black funereal wind,
my voice was lost and far away.
—No comfort in that smashed ravine,
no silver tips to contemplate away
the pain.
Just a hovering bird of prey,
a ruined sky,
above my grave."

Mexican Night at the Union Bar

I have stopped your car.
Hit the brakes.
The locks are popped and although
you are drunk, you have agreed
to come with me,
along the grey path,
down from the cliff,
past the bank of the river,
cooling its brow in dark currents.
Now you are sombrero'd up
draped in pinks,
the table festooned with drinks
and friends, your smile—towards me,
your loneliness parked
back up there, in the car
on the grey path cliff,
the siren sea below.
Your smile is towards me,
through tassels bouncing to ranchera,
tendril voices bursting orange and lime.
The room is dancing now,
bodies through air
trailing globes of light
absorbing night with young colour.
Chilies burn green vision
into your mouth.
It shows in your smile,
that you are every bit alive.
A whole world away,
—from that car,
those cliffs,
the wrecked sun against waves.
You are a whole world away.
You grip the wheel,
until there's just sky—
and a wasteland of stars.

Tip 7

Make your way boys
pick through the fade
—carrying
your grinding

breathless fear
in readiness beside you.
Down we go,
down the hill.

The darkest river
runs beside us,
this freezing rush,
as if to drag our

tiny pilgrims home.
Their tender bodies, gone.

Bodyless

Morning brings the yellow veil of grief
which hangs by day like vinegar in air
and soaks each night into my thirsty skin

On endless days I walk myself amongst
the green where feathered spores and seeds slip by
and closed buds hold life hostage in their silk

I listen for you nesting in the quills
aimless through this crumpled brow of land
hoping for your gentle sunbird sound

My layers peel, red-lined as fibres strip
the tender of my flesh gives way to light
bright flex muscle-sinew takes its flight

Spring rewound with backward blossom flows
as showers re-rained into sky above
and all the forest peels me from my bones

Yolk exposed to sharpness of its shell
reducing me to where the love is held
like wine, in the dark pocket of a mouth

Cool beck and bourn beneath the ache of sun
and as a river seeks its sovereign sea
I flow, I brim, I run and run and run

Flood

I can charge those floodgates
Hit the tempo and rest in place
The air can rush in and
Slam me down
I can run to black cliff
If I want
I can see its mouth
I can carry the empty
Body lost into air
Along the beach
Littered with
All those shrunken
Shells
Worn with holes
Half spirals and shine
I can lay that weathered vessel down
I can whisper, I can
Cast it out
To sea
In a tiny wooden boat

Funeral

Muscari and its fortune globes
have come to mourn and made
their homes amongst the
orange parrot tulips
flaming there—like open wounds.
And in the rustle
of their psalms, I yearn for your
forgotten arms—
The bells of birdsong
fall bereft upon the garden,
spring has left and summer didn't
leave a note to say
when it would follow.
In dark pews of anemones,
life hides itself from blossom
breeze, forget-me-nots splash
the place in blue-dust-longing for
your face, wishing in the wasted
sunshine for your missing shadow.

A Winter Morning

Wake in winter dark.
Wild dark. The kind of dark
that's waiting at the edge of things.

Feet bare, with wool bound shoulders
she walks like those
that walk upon the edge

of cliffs, on stormy days
in spray and screech of gulls,
the frantic obligation

of the sea below.
She walks like someone
on the edge of things.

The light is always first.
The arc of all.
The light was the beginning

and the end.
Standing. Feet bare, wool bound,
on the cusp of dawn,

she can see the sky
and things have more colour.
The colour blooms,

it takes the edge off things.
Tiny pieces of the light
settle in her hand.

Clay

After Katrina, New Orleans 2016

Standing behind a chain-linked fence,
two legs of stone, the Six Flags sign.
In early April, cool snap sun, I scaled that fence,
camera slung across the swallow inked into my skin.

I disturbed the silence of morning's sky
and a ferris wheel, its one lonely eye
drowned into a blue grief lake,
returned my gaze.

A lone wind wandered through the art deco O's
of a fallen high striker, the hit and ping of orange
against mauve and rusted steel on green.
I caught some movement in the changing light,

through windows rippled with bullet-hole-bullseyes
and grey thrown graffiti. I saw your outline
in film reel still, your face from shadow
as space filled between us.

In this void kingdom, looted by time,
we met again over someone's lost prize,
a flood damaged toy — its mud caked smile.
Later you posed to the click of my camera,

re-sounding the imprint of our past lives.
A moment framed in rotten wood,
bird call rising in reeling pitch,
this lonely wind-swept place, a bridge.

Ysbyty Ifan

Ancient backcloth upland moor, shifting with the currents of a restless wind
Beneath quiver-grass parched runnels, lie brass rubbings potted into ground
A bronze-agronomist cured and historied within glug and clag of peat-land bog

His green pool whispers flow through leather bones, chambered under-ground
Iterations rotted into earthtongues, gills and seeds. A carbon keep, embogged
We patch the purple-orange hummocks, so muddied river crossings can rewind

Time speckles gold upon the Plover, returns Whorl-Snails and sculpts the bog
Back to ewer. Stagnant moss births fruiting bodies, rafting spinner silk enwinds
With Sundews trapping raptors, feeding rooting bonnets. When earth regrounds

Upland bog. Oxidised Pitkins pink the wind, history sings through quenched ground.

Hatton Flight

'21 Locks, 45 meters, 2 miles,' you said,
walking ahead, so your voice trailed back.
'Stretching as far as St Mary's church.'
Its distant spire piercing the golden sky,
a page in picture book pose.

21 locks of waterway passage,
house boat chimneys,
wood-fire trails in air,
doll's-house velveteen glow
in windows. Timekeepers, teapots,
bandanna-necked dogs,
framed in October felted fog.
45 meters,
tide's eternal rise and drop.
clock-work through all seasons,
from swallow tails to frost.

2 miles down I noticed, then,
in one sweep of the lock's great arm,
everything that you had meant,
washed through
a swirling eddy of time.
And up ahead
in the dimming light,
a little girl— in silhouette,
balancing atop the gate,
windlass, waving in the air.
You walked ahead to the next lock
and left her   skipping there.

Reflections

Time sits with a book. The season
outside is rain. The roses are slept
and we must all be dressed by noon

Your blue collision
and sun-blast sends me scattered
into gull-flung air

Time listens for the sound, when the hush of warm
air is cloying in the gut. On slow mind days
the snap will come that opens your red voice.

The gasp of you on a bluster day
pulls at my hair,
you roll me over

I check for signs of damage in the shower.
The breasts are wrong. I should have had
them taken off. I leave them in a drawer for the estate.

I climb inside you, wade into your uprush,
brace for our attrition
am left floating in you for days

Voicing is a stretch—time needs a stitch.
I can mitigate and clip it with soft breath.
Am I too old to feed it blood and birth it to the page?

I listen for the others caught inside your teeth
We are distanced.
Your tidal paths, desire lines

My high arched pain, crouches low. Time bathes
an earnest wound with rage. I am flagrant shadow.
All at once it is the noon and I am fully clothed.

Homing

Wisteria pinks the window that you stare through,
waiting for him with small expectant hands against the pane.
A grey speckled racer comes in, slender on lilac rain.
Since he left, we count the garden birds each day
and this one has paired with a wood pigeon
who bobs in green sheen, plumps to her plum coo
where they nest.

She must have flown off course, diverted by his amber eye,
decided not to race again. Chose to leave her loft
in soft expectant gloom. Will she miss the illusory touch,
the magnetised brush of blue balm against her wings?
When winter comes to steal her mate and spill her squabs
will her thoughts return to the solenoid pulse
of summered-flight?

I watch you skip down the path with him.
She bears the rain, tending to her pale eggs
as I have brooded gifts inside regret.

'Araf deg mae mynd ymhell'

And she does go far, slowly
into blue spaces at the edge of sleep,
where she was young and tender,
borne through blood line tunnels
of peat and plant—liminal places
where she recalls her language.

Her tongue, a muted river, swept her mother
out of this world forever. She dreams
of shadows—the snap of leather and buckle,
the grind of earth and root. She holds
a still child, a bundle of sticks, some lost stones.
The unsaid pooling inside her head,

a leaking chapel, a well, a cave. She quarries
her loss, her mother hunger—her swallowed voice.

My Native Land, Goodnight

Nos da, to the melting hues of my mother's land.
Her voice is in scrub grass mountains,
the green of curled breath ferns.
The curve of her cheek is the carved valley,
—wildling face
dissolved in landscaped sky,
the old restless blue of cool-brow hills.

Nos da, to the Brecon wilds —echoed
with the red dust call of kites,
their spiralled paths to night, making
evening a song, that treads your black hills.
Cariad   mountain flower   secret dark.

To leave you here in sleep, is where I meet myself
Lie down with my bones, become earth, root, plant.

Acknowledgements

Thank you to the editors of the following publications who originally published the poems listed:

To My Country, Dreich— Summer Anywhere anthology
The Drowners— Green Ink Poetry
A Child— Brieflyzine
Flood— The Crank
Ysbyty Ifan— Magma Poetry
Homing, Choices Zine, Mum poem press, edited by Liz Berry
My Native Land Goodnight - Folklore Poetry

Special thanks to Matthew M C Smith from Black Bough Poetry and Maja Trolle.

About blood moon POETRY

blood moon POETRY is a small indie press and a home for women who write poetry. We feature poetry and illustrations by women from all walks of life, striving to support and amplify marginalised voices in particular. Seeking out new and undiscovered creative women, we specialise in the compilation, editing and publication of print poetry anthologies and pamphlets centred on themes of womanhood. Our bi-annual digital journal also features work from our growing online community of poets, authors and illustrators. We aim to celebrate the diverse beliefs, paths to and complex perspectives on womanhood by showcasing that diversity in our publications.

Connect with us on Instagram @bloodmoonpoetrypress
Find us and subscribe at www.bloodmoonpoetry.com

Printed in Great Britain
by Amazon

74912393R00041